The

Most

Beautiful

Gardens

Ever

Written.

The
Most
Beautiful
Gardens
Ever
Written.
A Guide

Jane Gillette

EDITIONS

Publishers of Architecture, Art, and Design

Gordon Goff, Publisher

www.oroeditions.com

info@oroeditions.com

Published by ORO Editions

Text: Jane Gillette

Graphic Design: Marc Treib

Proofreading: Sonya Mann

Managing Editor: Jake Anderson

10 9 8 7 6 5 4 3 2 1 First Editions

Library of Congress data available upon request.

ISBN: 978-1-935935-22-3

Color Separations and Printing: ORO Group Ltd.

Printed in China

"When you walk through the garden,
you better watch your back."

— Tom Waits

Profound thanks to:
Mary Fawcett,
who read innumerable versions
of this manuscript;
Sarita Govani and Monica Way,
who coped with
producing the images;
Marc Treib,
who helped with editorial, graphic,
and production guidance;
and Peter Walker,
who has provided
my landscape education.

The author has labored diligently to identify, locate, and contact rights holders, informing them of the intention to publish their work. Despite significant and reasonable efforts, in some cases it has been impossible to identify and make contact with rights holders. Should the author be contacted by rights holders following publication, steps will be taken in future publications to secure appropriate copyright permissions.

Introduction

This guidebook invites you on a tour of ten beautiful gardens. A tour? you say. No thanks. We answer: Relax. No need to get on a dreadful bus with a hoard of Garden Club ladies. No need to trudge through rain and heat to view plants that are frequently imperceptible. No need to struggle to hear the well-informed but distant guide explain the obvious. No, this guidebook merely suggests a tour of thousands and thousands of pages of beautiful fiction. All you have to do is settle into your favorite chair, in front of the fire or out on the back porch, and . . . read to your heart's content.

At the beginning and the end of this guidebook we will consider beautiful gardens in novels about love. In between, we will explore beautiful gardens that depict the stalker mentality, criticize the government, memorialize extravagance and stupidity, exhibit gentlemanliness, exemplify futility, make fun of the bourgeoisie, and record childhood anxiety and parental strife. We note that these novels generally have many unpleasant things to say about what is sometimes called "the client class."

In consulting this guidebook, please remember that the titular word "most" is hardly definitive and makes what is only a poetic claim to the exclusionary. "Beautiful" is always a personal opinion, and, happily, in addition to the hundreds of beautiful gardens that already exist in novel form, there is always room for another. Also please remember that this acclamation of beauty makes no claim whatsoever for design excellence. Nor do these gardens provide the experiential pleasure that is the main strength of the actual landscape: no scents, no sounds, no touch of sun and breeze on your skin. Above all, remember that no matter what plants, what garden features, what atmospherics are lauded in the texts, they are overwhelmed by the powerful manipulations of narrative and language. Ultimately, these gardens are beautiful because they express and intensify the meaning of the great novels in which they appear. Sadly—and happily—this means that these ten most beautiful gardens resonate with the stupidity, sadness, and evils of human life.

I.
The Garden of Polygamy

Murasaki Shikibu
The Tale of Genji

[Japan, circa 1000]

Genji's magnificent estate in Heian-kyo (modern-day Kyoto) consists of a mansion facing south across a fore-court of white sand toward a large artificial lake that stretches east-west and features an artificial island (I, 441–42). The house and garden cover four *cho* of land, some fourteen acres, large considering that one *cho*, 3.5 acres, was the usual size of an aristocrat's estate. We learn about the layout from scenes in which depicting garden design was not Murasaki Shikibu's primary motive.[1] Still, we can assume that the Rokujo-in corresponds in general design to the aristocratic Heian estates we know about from other sources. Its construction also reflects contemporary practices. For his managers Genji—the designer—picks "men of taste" from among the provincial governors, a powerful yet despised class to which Murasaki Shikibu herself belonged (I, 288). His servants would probably have done the actual work—although this is not clearly specified.[2]

The most beautiful thing about the garden of the Rokujo-in is that there is nothing natural about it, or, to be more precise, nothing merely natural, for every bit of nature in its confines comes enriched or burdened by symbolic meanings of several hundred years' standing. The young court ladies—the tale's initial audience—were, like its characters, part of a tight culture of 10,000 interrelated nobles who "read" every plant and every plant product (dye, fabric, food), every nuance of weather and season, every insect and animal, every form of land and water with reference to the body of poetry that dominated their lives. No social interaction was complete without a poem—no romantic encounter, no familial association. The novel includes some 800 poems and references hundreds and hundreds more; most contain a natural image, which in turn refers to natural images in many other poems. In such a literary treatment the garden becomes far more than the designed surrounds of a building.

Son of the emperor by a politically insignificant concubine, Genji is handsome, intelligent, rich, politically adept, proficient in all the arts, and a romantic marvel, for he is loyal to the numerous women with whom he has adventures. It is not until his middle years that he builds the Rokujo-in to shelter a number of these ladies whom he has acquired over twenty years of philandering, most of which took place at a distance from the imperial court in gardens dominated by weeds and a general state of decay expressing the status of their marginalized inhabitants. The following (incomplete) list suggests

Although Genji's Rokujo-in garden is a place of the utmost convention, it is also the site of Kaoru's epiphany about the transitory essence of the natural world.

the improbability of the women with whom Genji has
had affairs:

> Yugao *(poor)*
>
> the Akashi lady *(rustic)*
>
> Hanachirusato *(placid)*
>
> Suetsumuhana *(ugly and unaccomplished)*
>
> Utsusemi, the modest wife of a deputy
> provincial governor.

Genji's two great loves—who are related to and resemble
each other—are Fujitsubo, his father's consort, by whom
Genji secretly has a son who grows up to be the Reizei
Emperor, and Murasaki, whom Genji adopts when she
is not yet ten. Even though she is of insufficiently high
lineage to be his primary wife, she is the love of his life.
Genji eventually brings several of these ladies to reside
at the Rokujo-in.

At first Genji's mansion seems to offer salvation because
his supportive loyalty suggests a more or less rational
solution to the problem of institutional polygamy, the
pervasive practice by which the imperial court forged
aristocratic alliances. The Rokujo-in also alludes to the
practical need to control the female jealousy so common
in polygamous situations: It is named for its location in
the Sixth Ward on the former property of the Rokujo

Haven, whose wandering spirit—the creation of jealousy and wounded pride—kills Genji's love Yugao and Aoi, his primary wife.

And yet, despite those nods to the benefits of masculine loyalty and mutual feminine understanding, the Rokujo-in ultimately expresses "natural" support for institutional polygamy because it takes the form of a mandala aligned to the directional formulae of the imperial city and court, a pattern intensified by the seasonal affiliations of the individual ladies:

> *Southeast:* Murasaki (spring)
> *Southwest:* the daughter of the Rokujo Haven, Akikonomu, who becomes Empress (autumn)
> *Northwest:* the Akashi lady, whose daughter becomes empress (winter)
> *Northeast:* Hanachirusato (summer).

The author does make one significant change to this institutionally-mandated mandala. The south is the most important geomantic direction, and yet, despite her social unimportance, Murasaki's quarters are located in the southeast quarter—perhaps to emphasize the importance of romantic love.

Each garden is planted with seasonally and poetically appropriate plants. The length of this informative passage suggests that readers found such details interesting—horticulturally perhaps, but undoubtedly because of the accompanying symbolic meanings and poetic allusions, all hidden to us. Interestingly, the description follows neither the circular pattern of the mandala nor the order of the seasons:

> The southeast quarter boasted high hills, every tree that blossoms in spring, and a particularly lovely lake; and in the near garden, before the house, [Genji] took care to plant not only five-needled pines, red plums, cherry trees, wisteria, kerria roses, and rock azaleas, all of which are at their best in spring, but also, here and there, discreet touches of autumn. In Her Majesty's quarter he planted the hill already there with trees certain to glow in rich autumn colors, turned springs into clear streams, added rocks to the brook to deepen its voice, and contrived a waterfall, while on the broad expanse of his new-laid meadow, flowers bloomed in all the profusion of the season. The result was an autumn to put to shame the moors and mountains of Saga and Oi. The northeast quarter, with its cool spring, favored summer shade. Chinese bamboo grew in the near garden, to freshen the breeze; tall groves offered welcoming depths of shade, as in

a mountain village; the hedge was of flowering
deutzia; and among the plantings of orange,
fragrant with the past, of pinks and roses and
peonies, there also grew spring and autumn
flowers. The east edge of this quarter was divided
off into a riding ground with a pavilion and
surrounded by a woven fence. Sweet flag had
been induced to grow thickly beside the water,
for the games of the fifth month [the summer
Sweet Flag festival], and the nearby stables
housed the most superb horses. The northwest
quarter's northern sector was given over to rows
of storehouses. Along the dividing fence grew
a dense stand of pines intended to show off the
beauty of snow. There was a fence entwined with
chrysanthemums to gather the morning frosts of
early winter, a grove of deep-hued oaks, and a
scattering of nameless trees transplanted from
the fastnesses of the mountains (I, 402).

In contrast to the level of detail in this passage, Murasaki
Shikibu usually devotes far less space to describing the
physical garden than to the functions that take place
within it. In the first forty-five chapters the Rokujo-in
is firmly associated with the social life of the capital in
all its mingled complexity—private parties as well as

secular and religious celebrations rich in costume, decorative paraphernalia, and ritual. All emphasize a pervasive cultural appropriation of nature.[3] For example, two particularly important private events at the height of Genji's power are the concert to celebrate the New Year's mumming (I, 437) and an "imperial progress" to the Rokujo-in made by both the Reizei Emperor and the Retired Emperor Suzaku (I, 572–73).

In the last nine chapters, after the death of Genji, his Rokujo-in provides the never-forgotten contrast to the rustic villa on the Uji River, which is associated with true love, social isolation, and Buddhist religious belief and practice (rather than ceremonial ritual). The adventures of Genji's grandson Niou and putative son Kaoru—two of fiction's first anti-heroes—emblemize a critical attitude toward the romantic hero, polygamous marriage, and sexual passion itself. Kaoru is inspired to a higher vision, its anti-natural essence inferred (it would have been clear to Heian readers) by his reference to *Gosenshu* 1264—"That which they call this world lasts just the little while a mayfly lives, so briefly it might not be there at all" (II, 1073, note 41). He thinks about Uji and the sisters whom he and Niou have loved in that setting.

While he pondered that strangely painful tie on into the twilight, mayflies flitted before him in the air. "There it is, just there, yet ever beyond my reach, till I look once more, / and it is gone, the mayfly, never to be seen again." It might not be there at all, they say he murmured to himself (II, 1073).

So ineffable is Kaoru's epiphany of the fleeting natural world that it is merely reported as a rumor, a story: "they say." Yet even while his mind is drawn to the spiritual locale of Uji, his enlightenment takes place as he looks out into the beautiful garden Genji designed and built at the Rokujo-in.

II.
The Garden of Rejected Love

Francesco Colonna
Hypnerotomachia Poliphili:
The Strife of Love in a Dream

[Italy, 1499]

Colonna's idealized landscapes—especially the garden
Isle of Cytherea, home of Venus herself—are wondrous
concoctions of exhaustive description, what translator
Joscelyn Godwin appropriately calls "excess and super-
abundance" created by "grotesque accretion." The text
is accompanied by simple woodcuts that have served
for centuries as a veritable quarry of elements for actual
gardens. Godwin points to the sleeping nymph in the
forecourt of the Villa d'Este, the Venus Grotto of the
Boboli Gardens, some of the monsters at Bomarzo, and
the canals and marble colonnade at Versailles. John Dixon
Hunts sees the *Hypnerotomachian* influence in the Hortus
Palatinus in Heidelberg, Dumbarton Oaks, and designs
by Palissy and Cerceau.[4]

The useful presence of these design elements pleasantly
contradicts the madness of the narrative and reminds
us that Poliphilo's extended dream-construct can be
called a garden in its entirety. More literally it is a nightmare landscape studded with hallucinatory gardens. For
example, the Isle of Cytherea is composed of concentric
circles, an idealized form. It is a place of fertile abundance
with many, if not all, of the world's plants—or at least
those listed in Colonna's source, Pliny the Elder's *Natural
History*. By all rights the island home of Venus should

be a garden of pure pleasure. Alas! whether by incompetence or craft, it is not so. The chief problem, as well as the great delight, in visiting this specific garden, as well as the rest of Colonna's extended nightmare landscape, lies in trying to credit the writer with the correct degrees of ineptitude and skill. As a novelist he undermines himself on every page as he ridiculously, brilliantly forces the reader to experience a nightmare in which a lover (Poliphilo, the lover of Polia, that is, the lover of many things) moves through a ruined landscape toward an erotic experience with a woman who does not return his love. Poliphilo's obsessive desire, his deluded hopes, his never-quite-attained sexual satisfaction create a state of anxiety transferred to buildings, gardens, and artifacts (including women's clothing, shoes, and hair), all endlessly described in the first-person narrative voice of Poliphilo. By the time we reach the Isle of Cytherea—the ideal garden—we hold no hope for Poliphilo's happiness despite the optimistic doings of the plot. The only perfect garden would, after all, be one in which Polia returns Poliphilo's love.

The narrator's controlling sexual fantasy is conveyed by the altar to Priapus, who is significantly surrounded by a bevy of worshipping maidens.

We may first notice Colonna's paradoxically inept skill in the way his sources bleed through the text. From the first page we uneasily recognize scraps of Ovid, Apuleius, Pliny, and Vitruvius, a recognition that is, on the one

hand, awkward, on the other, perfect, for we see how Poliphilo's sleeping mind constructs a dream from the distorted fragments of his reading. Similarly, the plot seems threadbare—and yet we recognize it as the wishful thinking of Poliphilo's dream-construct. Hence, Book I —a first-person narration—follows Poliphilo to a ruin-strewn landscape where he meets Polia, who seems unusually friendly given what we've been told about Poliphilo's unrequited love. Together they travel first to the court of Queen Eleuterylida (Free Will) and then to the Isle of Cytherea. In both locations the dreamer concocts simpleminded rituals to insure that he and Polia will love each other with equal fervor. In Book II Polia seems to tell her side of the love story—with almost no description. We learn, however, that this too is part of Poliphilo's dream, one more problem with, or brilliant manipulation of, the narrative voice. At one point in Book II Polia delivers a first-person account of Poliphilo's side of the story in his first-person voice, which actually is his account within the dream of Polia's version of his voice and story (which does not quite gibe with his own account). Strategy after strategy— it is tempting to call them the products of a stalker mentality—insure that Poliphilo's wish to be loved by Polia will prevail in the dream-work. Did the obsessive novelist write this opus for some real-life Polia as an immense expression of a love she did not return?

Approximately 450 pages of Godwin's 475-page trans
lation consist of Poliphilo's exhaustive descriptions
of the various gardens and buildings he "sees" on his
journey. These descriptions are freighted with mean-
ingful allegories (never satisfactorily explained), fake
hieroglyphics (translated into banal nothings), and
smatterings of Arabic and Greek (masterpieces of the
trite). Similarly, every inscription in the woodcuts offers
us a commonplace posing as wisdom. The language
Colonna uses for the book emphasizes this paradoxical
tone of fraught but empty profundity: Italian syntax
with a Latin vocabulary.[5]

The extended as well as specific gardens of *Hypnerotomachia Poliphili* easily lend themselves to Freudian
interpretations that we strive honorably to ignore, and
yet Poliphilo's oft-stated praise of both mimetic realism
and classical antiquity suggests that some submerged
erotic connection between the proportions of the human
body and the classical orders drives his unceasing desire
to describe. The structural illogicality of the dream-work
is in itself Colonna's foremost strategy for creating reader
anxiety, but it is also worth noting two linguistic devices
he employs to create places he unreasonably claims are
beautiful: his insistence on the inadequacy of description
and his use of the negative comparison.

Every page of the novel revels in the failure of language.
As he describes and describes and describes, Polyphilo
repeatedly confesses his inability to describe. For example,
in the middle of a fifty-page description of the sacrifice
to Priapus, he confesses to failure (p. 177); before a
twenty-page description of Cupid's boat, he admits, "I
cannot properly describe everything that I was kindly
permitted to participate in by watching" (p. 277); at
the end of a twenty-five-page description of the temple
of the High Priestess, Poliphilo is distracted by Polia:
"Therefore forgive me, reader if I have not written at
full length about every detail" (p. 214); and in describing
the sacred fountain on Venus's garden island of Cytherea,
the sexually-fraught symbolic goal of Poliphilo's erotic
quest, he reneges:

> Each side was three feet wide, and the height
> from the golden base to the beam was seven
> feet. I think that the dignity and reputation of
> these things, with their miraculous and match-
> less workmanship, will be more appropriately
> served by my silence; therefore my description
> will be poor and meager (p. 361).

This device suggests there is much, much more to all
these places than we are being told. Yet we know Poliphilo's words ultimately fail because they correspond

to no reality, especially not to the one reality Poliphilo would like to establish beyond doubt: that Polia loves him. Another brilliant linguistic device, the negative comparison, occurs on virtually every page. One brief, vegetation-related example must suffice. In describing the capitals of a row of columns in the great portal Poliphilo tells us, "The over-refined Callimachus saw nothing like them in the acanthus growing from the basket upon the Corinthian maiden's tomb, which he expressed in his charming ornament" (p. 49). We know what the absent object—in this case Callimachus's Corinthian column—looks like; it is based on the acanthus. But not these present and ever-so-much-more-amazing columns! Thus Poliphilo seems to describe ineptly, while skillfully reminding us that the objects being described can't really be described because they don't exist.

Can any actual garden be as beautiful as this extensive expression of madness?

The Garden of Pornography

[T'ang Hsien-Tsu]
Chin P'ing Mei, or
The Plum in the Golden Vase

[China, 1618]

The essence of the novel is suggested by its title, comprised of one syllable from the names of three female characters, Gold Vase Plum, variously translated as *The Plum in the Golden Vase* or *The Glamour of Entering the Vagina*. The story tells of the rapid rise and fall (tumescence and detumescence) of Hsi-men Ch'ing, who dies from the ill effects of an aphrodisiac and is appropriately called a prick by everyone at his funeral. As translator David Tod Roy points out, the chance homophone of semen added to the proverbial sound of money tells the whole story.[6] Of these ten novels with beautiful gardens, the *Chin P'ing Mei* seems the least concerned with the glorious manipulations of language, a nevertheless clever stratagem that focuses attention on the materialistic world of Hsi-men Ch'ing.

In Chapter 14, Hsi-men decides to merge his property with the adjacent one, which belongs to his most-recently-acquired wife, Hua Li P'ing-erh. The new garden will sport "an artificial hill and a summerhouse" as well as a three-room belvedere to be called the Flower-viewing Tower (I, 295–96). To this end, Hsi-men turns over 500 taels of silver to his manager and head servant, who acquire "the necessary bricks, tiles, lumber, and stone" and then supervise construction (I, 325). For comparison pricing, a twelve-year-old girl could be bought for a mere four taels of silver (II, 373). Two months later, when the tower is nearing completion and the foundation for the summerhouse is under construction (I, 329), Hsi-men gets in trouble with the law, and building is interrupted until he can bribe the relevant officials. Later we learn that the summerhouse is conventionally and not very specifically named "the Hall of Assembled Vistas" (II, 203), another invitation to the voyeurism we both participate in and abhor.

After six months the new garden is complete, and Hsi-men's head wife invites the lesser wives to a "feast of wine and delicacies" (I, 377ff.). For five or six pages the novelist, presumed to be T'ang Hsien-tsu, author of *The Peony Pavilion*, describes the new garden in a series of poems and songs. The nature of the description leaves readers in some doubt about whether all these things really exist in the "actual" garden of the novel or only in poetic allusions to gardens in general. In either case these multitudinous features emphasize the material nature of a garden constructed as property. The garden includes:

> a red-lacquered memorial arch
> a crenellated wall of crushed limestone

"P'an Chin-lien Engages in a Drunken Orgy under the Grape Arbor" succinctly conveys the pornographic program of Hsi-men Ch'ing's garden, which the novelist delightfully elaborates in pages and pages of prose.

> a gate tower at the portal
> a grape arbor
> a juniper hedge
> many kiosks
> pavilions galore.

The text also mentions an ornamental T'ai-hu rockery, which serves as a location of revelry (II, 16, 140), serpentine streams and square pools, "frolicking fish," butterflies, swallows, and orioles. The highest point in the garden is the Cloud Repose Pavilion. Also mentioned are plantings of bamboo, pine, cypress, cedar, peach, palm, white plum, pomegranate, litchi, willow, crabapple, holly, and redbud. Throughout the novel great attention is paid to plants as symbols of women and love-making. Mention is made of lotus, water lily, chrysanthemum, daffodil, elecampane, dianthus, banksia, lilac, mimosa, caragana, yellow rose, jasmine, narcissus, plantain, helianthus, and peony.

The garden in the *Chin P'ing Mei* provides a beautiful example of the synecdochal type, a complicated indictment by an author who uses pornography to implicate the reader in the excesses he decries—and, above all, to escape political fury. Although Hsi-men's household presumably exists in the district town of Ch'ing-ho (Clear River), its real location is Beijing, for it is a microcosm of the imperial court during the recent reigns of the Chia-ching and Wan-li emperors of the Ming dynasty (1521 to 1566). To save his neck the novelist has carefully disguised his creation as a historical novel taking place during the twelfth-century reign of Emperor Hui-tsung. By the sixteenth century the novelist could safely criticize the collapse of the Northern Sung, at least if he masked his criticism in a heavily symbolic manner; thus Hsi-men is meant to be read as the emperor and his six wives as the "six traitors" (the evil ministers who were traditionally blamed for the fall of the Northern Sung). Roy points out that the term "six traitors" was also used as a metaphor for the senses. Well informed, imaginative readers could "re-translate" the presumably historical and conceivably philosophical pornographic novel into a criticism of the current dynasty.

Connoisseurs of today's product may find the pornography of the *Chin P'ing Mei* rather tame. On one outing, onlookers are significantly unable to tell if Hsi-men's wives are "noble," "imperial," or "whores" (I, 304). The three women of the title—two are wives, one an ambitious maid—live in the enlarged garden, where we readers look in on many styles of sexual intercourse, the murder of a child, and the endless eating and drinking of inappropriately luxurious fare. As for garden features, what we see most frequently are the Kingfisher Pavilion, which boasts an underground heating system and serves as the location for Hsi-men Ch'ing's homosexual romps, and the artificial hill, which contains a hidden whitewashed chamber for sexual sport named the Hidden Spring Grotto. Various sexual encounters reveal that the hill has a pavilion on its summit (no mention of view or prospect), while the Dripping Emerald Cavern lies halfway down, "where the flowering vegetation was at its thickest" (II, 145).

An infamous garden-related event provides a historical occasion for Hsi-men's illegal activity, one of T'ang Hsien-tsu's attempts to tie the microcosm of Hsi-men's household to the corrupt macrocosm of the Chinese state (albeit in a different dynasty): "The Flower and Rock Convoys" are transporting "the rare flowers and rocks required for the embellishment of the park. . . . But the water in the canal is low, and corvee laborers from eight prefectures have been requisitioned to tow the boats, with the result that: 'The officials are in dire straits, and / The people are reduced to destitution'" (IV, 124).[7] Hsi-men is promised that His Majesty will "'spend a great deal of money'" on "'Rare birds and unusual animals, / Chou vessels and Shang tripods, / Han censers and Ch'in burners, / The stone drums of King Hsuan . . . and rare antiques and relics of all kinds,'" some of which Hsi-men will be permitted to supply (IV, 618). In this, as in all the garden descriptions of the *Chin P'ing Mei*, T'ang Hsien-tsu emphasizes the acquisition and use of materials—a beautiful fictional (and pornographic) strategy for condemning a culture that lacks spiritual values.

The Garden of No Prospects

Cao Xueqin
The Story of the Stone,
or *The Dream of the Red Chamber*

[China, 1760]

The most beautiful thing about Prospect Garden is
that it affords no physical overview. Of the hundreds
and hundreds of pages of piecemeal description, one
passage in particular suggests the truth. When Jia Zheng
leads some gentlemen friends on a tour of the garden,
they enter via an artificial ravine: "After they had advanced
a few paces in a somewhat northerly direction, the
ravine broadened into a little flat-bottomed valley and
the stream widened out to form a pool. Gaily painted
and carved pavilions rose from the slopes on either side"
(I, 328–29).[8] The central issue addressed specifically and
ironically in Prospect Garden, from its name to virtually
every incident that takes place within its confines, is
humanity's enduring lack of perception. How appropriate,
then, that it be located in a valley.

Much of the action takes place in the garden built by
the Jia family at great expense for the visit of the Imperial
Concubine, a Jia daughter and sister of the hero Bao-yu.
Although heavily influenced by Hsi-men Ch'ing's garden
in the *Chin P'ing Mei*, Prospect Garden by contrast
houses the innocent Jia sisters, cousins, and maids and
provides the setting for a romantic struggle between
Bao-yu's two cousins who symbolize the ideal and
practical sides of woman, Lin Dai-yu and Xue Bao-chai.

It is also the place where the siblings and cousins experience elegant poetry contests and heartwarming childhood revelry. In this fashion the garden expands the trope that identifies the briefly blooming maiden with the flower, not only by the fleeting quality of their existence but also by their unrealized potential. The maidens of the Jia family slowly approach their fertile years, and the garden, which seems destined to be a productive agricultural site, inspires endless manipulations and quarrels, all inspired by greed; whole chapters revolve around theft. As the family's financial problems grow more evident, the girls enter various unhappy marriages (in the form of patrilocal exogamy). They die and the garden decays. Superstition takes over. Rumors of monsters and ghosts frighten off the caretakers. "Plants were left untended, trees unpruned, and all the flower-beds unwatered" (V, 71–72). Soon the garden is a wilderness. Robbers kill the resident Buddhist nun. No one will buy Prospect Garden from the Jias. The Emperor won't even accept it as a gift. As destruction engulfs the whole clan, Prospect Garden becomes a microcosm of the imperial court and, thus, the empire.

The novel is autobiographical. According to its translator David Hawkes, Cao, an accomplished landscape artist

The poetry contests enjoyed by Jia siblings and cousins take place in pavilions similar to this one at Prince Gong's eighteenth-century estate in Beijing. Prospect Garden suffers such disrepair as the girls sicken and die.

who specialized in rock painting, spent his last impoverished years in Beijing's Western Hills, drinking heavily. Prospect Garden—a landscape exclusively composed of words—is not only the site of the lost golden world of adolescence; it is also the immeasurably splendid past from which the writer has fallen, a megalomaniacal pipe dream. To this end Cao mixed up the various generations of his family, changed the sites of their rise and fall (Nanking to Beijing), and "upgraded the family's importance."[9]

Extravagance in garden building must have been common because so many philosophical and religious traditions repeatedly warn against it. Andrew Plaks points out that the garden concept is consistently "used to convey the idea of extravagance, ostentation, or unwisely deployed resources" in the tradition of Confucian exegesis.[10] The Jias clearly fail to heed the warnings. We learn that Prospect Garden will cost at least 50,000 taels (I, 317) at a time when, according to Grannie Liu, a virtuous old lady who lives on a Jia family farm, twenty taels can support a peasant family for a year (II, 265). As for design, "the conception as a whole and the designs for its execution were alike the work of a well-known landscape gardener familiar to all and sundry by the sobriquet of 'Horticultural Hu,'" a description that suggests he can be relied on to do the absolutely conventional thing (I, 319). As for building, "before they started on the construction of this Garden, they made a very detailed drawing of the layout. It was only an artist's impression, but the measurements shown on it were all accurate'" (II, 339)—very accurate, very detailed, and amplified ironically by hundreds of pages of description in the form of three complete tours, of which the first is particularly important.

When Jia Zheng, the bureaucratic Confucius-spouting father, leads his friends through the ravine into the valley of the new garden, he encourages them to come up with poetic quotations that can be inscribed on boards or walls or gates, an absolutely necessary feature in which language emblemizes the obvious. In order to show that the garden is a typical product of the culture and a thoroughly social construct, Cao follows a pattern in depicting the various garden features, which include a five-frame gate-building and several vaguely-described miniature mountains with no indication of views from their summits. First, Cao describes the feature in physical terms. Next, Jia Zheng mouths a conventional platitude, and either he or one of his gentlemen friends suggests a

name and lines from a traditional Chinese poem. Then
Bao-yu criticizes the choice and offers a more appropriate
one, which will be validated by the Imperial Concubine
when she makes her tour. As a result readers see Prospect
Garden through a haze of traditional Chinese poetry—
an art that can be as thoroughly conventional as Horticultural Hu's garden design. Two more tours follow, one
by the Imperial Concubine, the other by Grannie Liu.
And yet, the more the garden is described, the more
surely readers remain lost. Language confuses rather
than clarifies. In later chapters, even when readers are
on occasion located firmly in the pavilions where the
various women live, the areas in between remain con-
fusing, and the garden always seems much larger than it
can possibly be, even if traversed by women with bound
feet.[11] In practical terms this vagueness permits Cao to
add pavilions or follies whenever the story demands. It
also suggests that the essential symbolic form of Prospect
Garden is a maze in which the ignorant Jia family wanders,
lost and confused.

Nature-based *objets d'art*, celebrations, and beliefs appear
on every page. Even while Cao provides evidence of
decadent extravagance, he clearly loves every *objet* and
cherishes every celebration—all reminders of the glorious,

albeit enhanced, past. The nature-based beliefs, although treated kindly, never rise to the level of philosophy in the characters' minds. They are merely delusions that make everyone feel better. Still, like the *objets* and *fêtes*, these beliefs contribute to our understanding of the Jias' luxurious lifestyle and their high valuation of good taste. In the end culture has swallowed nature, and it has done so in a beautiful fashion, but it is all to no avail. The beautiful irony of Prospect Garden is that, although artificial, it is—like every garden—subject to the natural processes of decay and death . . . as are its inhabitants.

The Garden of Gentlemanly Reticence

Laurence Sterne
The Life and Opinions of Tristram Shandy, Gentleman

[England, 1759–1767]

Of all the gentlemen in English literature perhaps the most loveable is Tristram's Uncle Toby. And yet his enclosed garden could easily serve as a symbol of the deluded and isolated mind, for it is defined by Uncle Toby's excessive innocence and shadowed by the difficulties of communication. These difficulties are what make his garden so beautiful.

Uncle Toby's life changed abruptly in 1695, during the Nine Years' War, when he was struck in the groin by a stone, "broke off by a ball from the parapet of a hornwork at the siege of Namur" as he stood "before the gate of St. Nicolas, in one of the traverses of the trench, opposite to the salient angle of the demi-bastion of St. Roch" (p. 55).[12] Provided with a map, he "could at any time stick a pin upon the identical spot of ground where he was standing when the stone struck him" (p. 68). However, when he returns to England, he has a great deal of trouble explaining "where and what he was about." He acquires a useful map, and "the more my uncle Toby pored over his map, the more he took a liking to it," for it provides a picture of reality that is refreshingly clear. Hence, during his recovery Uncle Toby collects other maps of fortified towns in Italy and Flanders, "carefully collating therewith the histories of their sieges, their demolitions, their improvements and new works." When Corporal Trim comes up with the idea of actually building the plans, Uncle Toby, blushing with pleasure, rushes off to Shandy Hall "with more heat and expectation" than a lover to a mistress (pp. 78–80).

The rood and a half of ground at the bottom of Uncle Toby's kitchen garden is cut off by a tall yew hedge and protected on the other three sides "by rough holly and thickset flowering shrubs," one of which seems to become a hornbeam hedge over the course of the novel. (In terms of land area a rood is a British unit equal to a quarter of an acre.) The soil contains just enough clay to facilitate the molding of angles but not so much as to cling to the spade (pp. 80, 367, 369). This space is the bowling green where Uncle Toby and Corporal Trim build models of the besieged towns of the War of the Spanish Succession (1701–1714). As soon as the plan of each invested town is known, Uncle Toby enlarges it "upon a scale to the exact size" of the bowling green and then transfers it "by means of a large role of pack-thread, and a number of small piquets driven into the ground." He then takes "the profile of the place, with its works, to determine the depths and slopes of the ditches" and, setting Trim to work, sits nearby and chats with

Maps, model-building, and words serve over the years to obscure the exact nature of the injury to Uncle Toby's groin at the 1695 siege of Namur. Do images of such fortifications as this construction by Vauban, circa 1674, continue to lurk in Uncle Toby's unconscious?

him "upon past-done deeds" (pp. 367-68). The bowling-green models of the besieged towns thus begin as attempts to explain the reality of war and sustain the healing of a physical wound. They end as a system unto themselves, an obsession that only serves to deepen confusion. To this end, Stern generously sprinkles the text with terms of fortification, which serve to baffle the reader, now as then. The intractability of language ultimately becomes the subject of the bowling green: Reality, apparently, cannot be expressed in words, but must be represented by material means that clarify and miniaturize and distance. In this guise man can exercise control over reality. What a beautifully ironic message for a great novel!

Throughout we are given glimpses of Uncle Toby's "hobby-horse" and treated to various accidents within the boundaries of the fortifications (the wandering cow, the bridge destroyed by lovers). Slightly more than midway through the novel, we are told more about their methods of building the model as we are treated to a year-by-year account of the War of the Spanish Succession reduced to physical improvements. In 1701, "the first year's campaign," Uncle Toby and Trim set up their process. They receive the accounts of the war from the daily papers, then proceed with the siege on the side of the allies: "And when the face of a bastion was battered down, or a defense ruined,—the corporal took his mattock and did as much,—and so on" (p. 369). In the second year "my uncle Toby took Liege and Ruremond," and the pair adds a sentry box for rainy days (pp. 369–70). In 1703 they add a "little model of a town" so that it will seem as if they are actually besieging something. Uncle Toby insists that it be built in the style of Flanders with every house independent so that they can move them about as they wish. In 1705 they add a church with a steeple; in 1708 or so Trim creates an elaborate effect of continual firing; and with the Treaty of Utrecht in 1713 they dismantle Dunkirk. Uncle Toby's re-created sieges bring pleasure "from the consciousness we both had, that in carrying them on, we were answering the great ends of our creation" (p. 382). The pair continues to build models of all the little disturbances that continue to disrupt Europe in the years after the war proper has been concluded, for example the siege of Messina in 1719.

All this model-building culminates in one wonderful miscommunication: The Wadman Affair. Long before Freud, Sterne pointed out that although our every thought is shadowed by sex, we lack an accurate terminology and are frequently embarrassed to use the inadequate

one we have. The bowling green is located next to the
Widow Wadman's house and garden—edged by a
hedgerow on his side and a thickset arbor (perhaps
recalling pubic hair) on hers. This barrier provides
Uncle Toby with some protection until the building of
a vaginal sort of wicker gate leaves him at the Widow's
mercy. He "falls in love" but is innocent of and uninter-
ested in sex to a degree we may now tend to interpret,
perhaps incorrectly, as repressed homosexuality. When
Uncle Toby fails to pursue in a sexual fashion, the Widow
Wadman's suspicions (mistakenly) fall on the injury to
his groin. It is only natural "for Mrs. Wadman . . . to wish
to know how far from the hip to the groin; and how far
she was likely to suffer more or less in her feelings, in the
one case than in the other." Can he do it? At last she asks:

> —And whereabouts, dear Sir, quoth Mrs. Wadman,
> a little categorically, did you receive this sad blow?
> —In asking this question, Mrs. Wadman gave a
> slight glance towards the waistband of my uncle
> Toby's red plush breeches, expecting naturally, as
> the shortest reply to it, that my uncle Toby would
> lay his fore-finger upon the place.

However, Uncle Toby calls for his large map of the town
and citadel of Namur and its environs, takes Mrs. Wadman's
hand, and with "virgin modesty laid her finger upon

the place"—on the map (p. 535). The Widow Wadman is too decent to protest this miscommunication, and ultimately Trim must explain to Uncle Toby what she was actually asking—a question that seems unreasonably salacious to this beautifully innocent gentleman.

Maps, we see, use abstraction to lead us a safe step away from reality. As do models. As do beautiful words.

The Garden of the Test Tube

Johann Wolfgang von Goethe
Elective Affinities

[Germany, 1808]

At some point after the French Revolution, four characters tirelessly "improve" the landscape of an estate somewhere in Germany. In doing so they beautifully act out Goethe's great question: Do human beings—unlike the rest of nature—possess free will, specifically when they are in the grip of sexual infatuation, the "natural" impetus to reproduce one's kind? Eduard and Charlotte are married, each for the second time. Eduard invites his oldest friend, the Captain, to join them on their estate. Charlotte invites her niece Ottilie. Eduard and Ottilie fall in love with each other, as do Charlotte and the Captain. Various disasters ensue in a contrived plot that reads not unlike the recording of a chemical reaction. The four begin with a strong belief in free will and end by believing they are not in control of their choices, variously blaming Providence, Fate, God, a malevolent spirit, the Zeitgeist, their physical surroundings. For most of the novel they behave as if they are the equivalents of chemical elements interacting in a laboratory experiment for which the garden beautifully provides the test tube. As the reaction takes place, the elements speed up, and the salient aspect of the estate landscape becomes the web of paths on which the characters move to and fro, up and down, back and forth across the landscape, all but "foaming over the brim" (p. 49).[13]

Throughout the novel the characters struggle to gain an overview. What they see, however, is usually just more of the estate and village. Although Goethe describes bits and pieces, he makes it almost impossible to envision the setting as a whole. Like the characters, the reader is embedded within the landscape. If the estate is so important, why doesn't Goethe simply sketch out the whole thing right at the beginning? Because there is nothing like an overview—and knowing where we are— to create a feeling of superiority. Conversely, there is nothing like being dislocated, especially within a landscape known to others, to make us feel unintelligent, humble, and helpless—just part of the scene. It is certainly much more difficult to believe in the existence of a superior, separate, and designing God and intelligent, free human beings in the face of a location that so successfully resists description and comprehension.

The Red Books of Humphry Repton lurk behind Goethe's gardens. What improvements did Repton imagine as he surveyed the landscape in this provocative illustration on his business card?

Throughout the account of their marital difficulties, the four spend much of their energy modifying the estate landscape as Goethe creates an uneasy parallel between these activities: Landscape gardening like marriage is a cultural activity that converts nature to human use. Each character interacts with the landscape in characteristic fashion. Eduard sees himself as the owner of his property,

eagerly pressing his desires on everyone else, confident
that he and nature think as one, even when nature proves
otherwise. (When we first encounter Eduard, for example,
he is grafting young trees, and we later learn that the
grafts don't take.) Charlotte is a small-scale improver,
managerial in part because she is so anxious. The practical
Captain prepares a map of the whole estate, which
presumably enables Eduard (but not, alas! the reader) to
see the landscape whole. Ottilie contributes to destruction with her every move. Eduard and Charlotte's baby
dies in her care, and one evening as they are looking at
the map she tells Eduard where she would place the
new pavilion. Delighted with her suggestion, he draws
a "crude and emphatic oblong on the ridge." Of course
this oblong doesn't destroy the map or its function, only
the Captain's pride: "It pained him to see his careful
and neatly drawn map disfigured" (p. 53). We note that
all four view productive agriculture as a distant managerial problem—how to make money out of tenant farms—
and even though their conscious landscape schemes fail,
the estate is still solvent at the end of the tale.

As for design, we know that the new landscape is "naturalistic," suggesting those designed by Humphry Repton.
Eduard and the Captain consult what, in the words of

the characters, seem to be Red Book-like "'volumes on English country houses'" with "'engravings'" (p. 46), before-and-after views of an "improved" landscape. When they open the volumes "they saw for each case an outline of the terrain and drawings of the landscape in its first rough and natural state, then on other pages depictions of the changes wrought on it by art in such a way as to utilize and enhance all the good already present there." The Reptonian quality of the improvements is suggested by the summerhouse folly, the edges of the lake, and the whole-hearted approval of a visiting Englishman (who comes from the Land of Naturalism). But the clearest evidence of the "naturalistic" style of the new garden comes from its stated if not described contrast to the formal style of Eduard's father's garden, created less than twenty years earlier.

The exact physical connections between the old and the new gardens remain unclear throughout the novel; we know more about them as contrasts in style (formal and Reptonian) and historical generations (father and son) than as specific geographical entities. Still, it is clear that the improvements to Eduard's estate are additions to an already designed landscape. The old and the new gardens exist side by side, the trees of the old gardens producing

better fruit than Eduard's new grafts. Why doesn't Goethe
have the new garden replace the other, since the destruction of the old in serial landscape design would parallel
divorce in serial monogamy? Because the question is
more interesting than the answer. Two scenes summarize
the problems with landscape improvement. In the first
Charlotte, discussing the two gardens, establishes garden
design as the product of the Zeitgeist. In the second the
visiting Englishman reveals that he has abandoned his
own much-improved estate to spend all his time on the
road because his son has expressed complete indifference
to his prospective property: "'It is certain that we spend
far too much time and money merely preparing to live.
Instead of settling down at once in a moderate condition
of life we go on and on expanding, to our greater and
greater discomfort'" (p. 183). These scenes suggest that
the best father and son can do is allow each other's gardens
to exist side by side and promote a historical awareness
that accepts new design and old as equal sources of
design values—a historic preservation ethic formulated
a century and a half before its time.

Nothing in this novel suggests that humanity has any
unusual extra-natural power aside from the ability to
concoct metaphorical excuses for powerlessness, a point

emphasized by the tireless landscape-improvement activities that accomplish no discernable improvement. And yet, faced with boredom and the vacuum of disbelief, the characters continue to work on the landscape, an activity that Goethe seems to hold in no more scorn than the other human behaviors noted in the text:

> organizing travel diaries
> playing the flute
> dressing up the villagers
> collecting architectural artifacts
> playing charades
> doing good
> giving parties
> buying new horses
> buying new dresses
> staging religious rituals
> setting off fireworks
> rowing on the lake
> celebrating birthdays
> practicing the fine arts
> making money
> practicing serial monogamy.

VII.

The Garden of Childhood Anxiety

Lewis Carroll
Alice's Adventures in Wonderland
and *Through the Looking-Glass and
What Alice Found There*

[England, 1865, 1872]

The first fictional garden many of us encounter lies at
the bottom of a rabbit hole and, though beautiful, it is a
far from happy place. Alice comes to rest slightly behind
the White Rabbit in a little hall. There, behind a low
curtain, through a door some fifteen inches high, she
spies "the loveliest garden you ever saw. How she longed
to get out of that dark hall, and wander about among
those beds of bright flowers and those cool fountains, but
she could not even get her head through the doorway"
(p. 12).[14] A desirable, but unattainable place, this garden
sets a direction to Alice's dream anxiety: If only she could
get there! First too big, then too small, next too big, she
asks the ultimate question—"Who am I, then?"—and
finds herself swimming in a pool of her own tears. Only
after many nonsensical adventures does she find herself
"among the bright flower-beds and the cool fountains"
(p. 68). And then, before she can enjoy this beautiful
place, she discovers it is also the Queen of Heart's croquet-
ground, where a trio of gardeners—the Five, Seven, and
Two of Spades—are painting a white rose-tree red. The
gardeners—they must be gardeners because they have
spades—have planted the wrong color, and heads are
about to roll.

In the sequel Alice comes upon another beautiful garden:
"a large flower-bed, with a border of daisies, and a willow-

tree growing in the middle" (p. 135). The flowers in the Looking-glass Garden speak their minds (which are decidedly unpleasant), criticizing in short order Alice's intelligence, complexion, and hair. The (presumably white or pinkish) Rose comments, "'Said I to myself, "Her face has got some sense in it, though it's not a clever one!" Still you're the right colour, and that goes a long way.'" Similarly the Tiger-lily opines: "'If only her petals curled a little more, she'd be all right'" (pp. 136–37). Alice derails their criticism by asking if they're frightened at "'being planted out here, with nobody to take care of you?'" Rose and Lily point to the protective tree, who can warn of danger by barking ("Bough-wough!"). They do, however, grow far more polite when Alice threatens to pick them. After they explain why they can talk (their flowerbed is so hard they can't sleep), Alice utters one of those polite phrases mouthed in order to appease testy people: "'I never thought of that before!'" and the flowers, sensing weakness, turn spiteful again: "'I never saw anybody that looked stupider,' a Violet said, so suddenly, that Alice quite jumped; for it hadn't spoken before" (p. 138). The Rose comments in a "kindly" fashion, "'You're beginning to fade, you know—and then one ca'n't help one's petals getting a little untidy.'"[15] Alice doesn't like this comment at all, not surprisingly since it foretells her imminent death.

"Oh, Tiger Lily," said Alice, "I wish you could talk!" In the bed of talking flowers a horrible rosebush blooms with the faces of little girls who look not unlike Alice herself.

The unpleasant conversation ends when the Larkspur announces, "'She's coming! . . . I hear her footsteps, thump, thump, along the gravel-walk.'" The Red Queen! When Alice explains that she "'only wanted to see what the garden was like,'" the governess-like Queen one-ups her: "'When you say "garden"—I've seen gardens compared with which this would be a wilderness'" (p. 140). Isn't this nonsense—a garden that is so ungardenlike as to be a wilderness? Doesn't the word "garden" exclude the quality of wilderness? Not in the syntax of comparison, as the Queen's statements prove. Poetry, games, language, logic itself are the productions of human consciousness, and all are laughed into insignificance during Carroll's investigation.

The garden is the scene of human consciousness transferred intact to mean-spirited (and highly cultivated) flowers, who become unpleasantly humanlike because they are able to speak. But when Alice escapes language and logic, she enters, for a few moments, an idyllic state. In contrast to the garden Alice finds the wood "where things have no names" both pleasant and without meaning: "'Well, at any rate, it's a great comfort,' she said as she stepped under the trees, 'after being so hot, to get into the—into the—into what?' she went on, rather

surprised at not being able to think of the word." More-
over, she cannot remember her own name. Again she
confronts and fails to answer the ultimate question:
Who am I?

> Just then a Fawn came wandering by; it looked
> at Alice with its large gentle eyes, but didn't seem
> at all frightened. "Here then! Here then!" Alice
> said, as she held out her hand and tried to stroke
> it; but it only started back a little, and then stood
> looking at her again.
> "What do you call yourself?" the Fawn said
> at last. Such a soft sweet voice it had!
> "I wish I knew!" thought poor Alice. She
> answered, rather sadly, "Nothing, just now."

They stroll through the wood, "Alice with her arms
clasped lovingly round the neck of the Fawn," until they
emerge into a field:

> And here the Fawn gave a sudden bound into the
> air, and shook itself free from Alice's arm. "I'm
> a Fawn!" it cried out in a voice of delight. "And,
> dear me! you're a human child!" A sudden look of
> alarm came into its beautiful brown eyes, and in
> another moment it had darted away at full speed
> (pp. 152–53).

When fawn and child forget who they are—a denial of consciousness symbolized by the darkness of the wood "where things have no names"—they can embrace. When they regain self-consciousness, Paradise is lost once again.

The Alice novels are doubly popular because of the illustrations by John Tenniel, who drew them with a great deal of input from Carroll.[16] Interestingly enough, all of the drawings that touch on the garden—or show some sort of non-forest vegetation—express significantly unpleasant situations. In *Alice's Adventures in Wonderland* Alice hides behind some sort of thistle and distracts a gigantic, dangerously playful puppy with a stick; backed by some sort of flower, she discovers the hookah-smoking Caterpillar; and later she stands before the same flower holding the pig / baby; the three hapless gardeners paint the white rose-tree red; and in the most fully depicted garden scene the Queen of Hearts points her finger straight at Alice and yells, "Off with her head!" In *Through the Looking-Glass* Alice looks bewildered as she stares at the talking flowers and the horrible rosebush, which blooms with the faces of little girls, faces that are not unlike Alice's. The Fawn in Alice's arms is, by contrast, a scene of gentle pleasure. Both have forgotten the word for myself.

As they stroll through the wood Alice lovingly clasps her arm around the Fawn's neck.

The Garden of Stupidity

Gustave Flaubert
*Bouvard and Pécuchet
with The Dictionary of
Received Ideas*

[France, 1880]

In 1841, thanks to an inheritance, two middle-aged
Parisian copy-clerks move to a small manor house and
garden with an outlying farm in Chavignolles, Normandy,
and even though we are supposed to laugh at their ensuing
attempts to achieve beauty and meaning, something
about the very nature of gardening elicits our sympathy:
Yes, they are stupid and, yecch!, they are us.

Even before Bouvard and Pécuchet acquire a property,
they buy gardening implements and imagine themselves
productively and romantically pruning roses while they
observe others performing the more strenuous chores. In
the garden they encounter a "plaster lady" coyly holding
up her skirt, and Bouvard's witticism—"Oh, excuse me!
Don't mind me!"—amuses them so much they repeat it
for years (pp. 32–39).[17] With similar dimwitted simplicity,
they expend great effort to no end, actively pruning,
weeding, and attacking pests. They plant "a peony in the
middle of the lawn and tomatoes, which were meant
to hang down like chandeliers, beneath the hoop of the
arbour." They create a compost heap and gather horse
dung from the roads. At first things look promising (p. 41).
Soon, however, beans, strawberries, tomatoes, broccoli,
aubergines, turnips, watercress, cabbages, and melons
fail for one reason or another.

Pecuchet plants "passion-flowers in the shade, pansies in the sun," covers "the hyacinths with manure," destroys "the rhododendrons through excessive chopping," stimulates "the fuchsias with glue," and roasts "a pomegranate tree by exposing it to the kitchen fire." They smother the honeysuckle under "paper domes well smeared with tallow," use huge props for the dahlias, stunt a japonica, and fail with Indian lilacs, Chinese roses, and eucalyptus (pp. 46–47). Similar efforts to grow pears, peaches, cherries, plums, and apricots for profit come to naught, leaving only a failed support system: "Strips of lath on the wall represented candelabras. Two posts at each end of the flower beds held up the horizontal wires tightly; and in the orchard, hoops showed the structure of vases, cones, pyramids" resembling "the parts of some unknown machine or the frame of a pyrotechnic showpiece." Despite the demands of their gardening books, they find it impossible "to obtain a perfect rectangle or an espalier, with six branches on the right and six on the left, not counting the two main ones, all in a fine fishbone pattern" (pp. 53–54). A hailstorm finishes off this blighted enterprise.

Before they buy a property Bouvard and Pécuchet carefully acquire tools for their gardening enterprise. So many tools are necessary to keep nature under control.

The hapless pair now moves from the practical to the artistic, guided by Pierre Boitard's *Garden Architect*, which prescribes a "horizon of marvels":

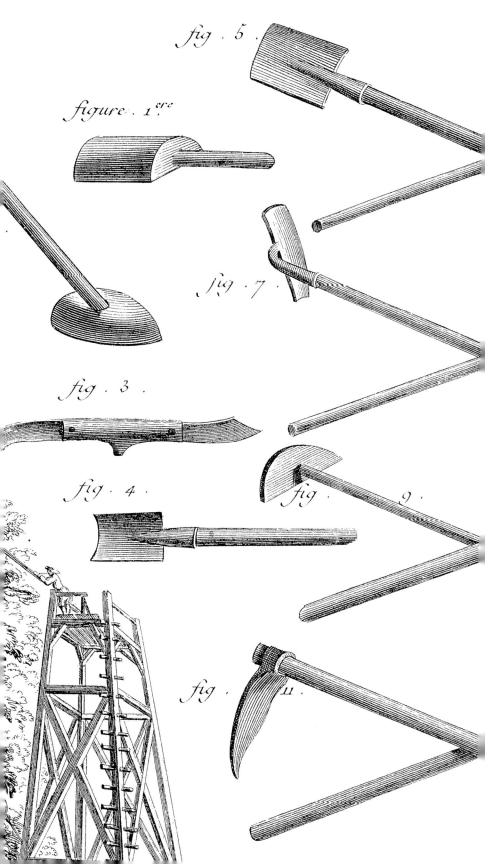

fig . 5 .

figure . 1ere

fig . 7 .

fig . 3 .

fig . 4 .

fig . 9 .

fig . 11 .

the melancholy and romantic garden—
"immortelles, ruins, tombs, and 'an ex-voto to
the Virgin, marking the place where some lord
has been struck down by a murderer's sword'"

the terrible garden—"hanging rocks, shattered
trees, burnt-out huts"

the exotic garden—"Peruvian torch-thistles"
which "evoke 'memories in a colonist or traveller'"

the solemn garden—"a temple to philosophy"
like Rousseau's Ermemonville

the majestic garden—"obelisks and triumphal
arches"

the mysterious garden—"moss and caves"

the meditational garden—"a lane"

the fantastic garden—"a wild boar, a hermit,
several sepulchers and a boat which unmoored
itself from the bank and took you into a boudoir
where jets of water soaked anyone who sat on
the sofa" (pp. 56–57).

What are poor home-owners to do when faced with so
many rich possibilities?

Bouvard and Pécuchet eliminate a few features as imprac-
tical and settle for

an arbour with a view of the copse, "which was
full of winding paths like a maze"

an espaliered wall that creates an archway to
reveal the perspective and, when the arch falls
reveals "a huge gap with ruins on the ground"

an Etruscan tomb, "a black plaster quadrilateral,
six foot high, resembling a dog kennel, flanked
with four dwarf firs"

a Rialto-like Venetian bridge straddling a pool
with mussel-shell-embellished edges and no
water

a rustic cabin with stained glass

a "vine-clad mound" with six "squared" trees
that support a Chinese pagoda, described as "a
tin hat with turned up points"

granite pieces from the Orne River, broken up,
numbered, transported in a cart, cemented
together, and piled up in the middle of the lawn
to create a rock that looks "like a gigantic potato"

the biggest lime-tree in the arbour, cut down and laid across the length of the garden "to convey the impression that it had been brought there by a torrent or struck down by lightning"

yews shaped like pyramids, cubes, cylinders, stags, armchairs, and peacocks

and, as a nod to the exotic, a field gate covered with plaster and embellished with "500 pipe bowls, representing . . . negroes, naked women, horses' hooves and snails," as well as Abd-el-Kader, the dey of the native chiefs of Algiers, which was invaded by France during this period.

"Like all artists they need applause," so Bouvard and Pécuchet give a dinner-party and at the end dramatically draw back the curtains to reveal their creation: "In the half-light it was quite dreadful," and, worse yet, no one understands it (pp. 57–61). They wisely blame the intellectual limitations of their guests.

This garden hosts a decade of bourgeois enthusiasms. Bouvard and Pécuchet have their evening cocktails on the mound. When they study history they read Thiers on the Revolution in the garden, its peaceful setting a contrast to "the thudding of the guillotine" (p. 119).

They use the garden as part of an unsuccessful mnemo-technic system (p. 122). When they take up sex, they flirt with their possible "beloveds" in the garden. Practicing gymnastics, they use the fallen lime-tree as a horizontal bar and replant the buttress of an espalier for a vertical bar. In its confines they try rope-straddling, rock-throwing, and stilt-walking (pp. 183–85). They take up various forms of healing, and their experiments with magnetism involve hugging a pear-tree. When a dog's corpse brings on thoughts of suicide, they experience a religious conversion. On Christmas Day they stroll "in their garden, breathing in the warm air, happy to be alive." In later years Pécuchet dresses in a monk's habit and digs in the garden, combining "manual labour with religious exercises" (pp. 222–26). They adopt two poor orphans, Victor and Victorine, and try to teach them geography by using sand and a watering-can to demonstrate rivers, islands, and gulfs. In so doing, they sacrifice "three flower-beds for the three continents" (p. 262). And when Victor boils his pet in a saucepan, they bury "the poor cat in the garden, under the pagoda" (p. 270).

Flaubert makes numerous garden entries in the appended *Dictionary of Received Ideas*, including:

> Cedars—"The one at the Botanical Garden was brought over in a hat"

Grottoes with Stalactites—"During the Revolution, Mass was celebrated there in secret"

Lilac—"Delights the heart because it means summer is near"

Palm Tree—"Supplies local color"

Plant—"Always cures those parts of the human body that it resembles"

Ruins—"Induce reverie; make a landscape poetic"

Sacrilege—"It is sacrilege to cut down a tree"

Site—"Place for writing poetry"

Summer-house—"Place of bliss in a garden"

Versailles—"A splendid idea of Louis Philippe's"

Windmill—"Looks well in a landscape."

Most of these idiocies spring from Romantic notions of gardening. Some are still current—for example, "Gardens (English) More natural than French ones."

How wonderful to make fun of the bourgeoisie by simply addressing their garden philosophies.

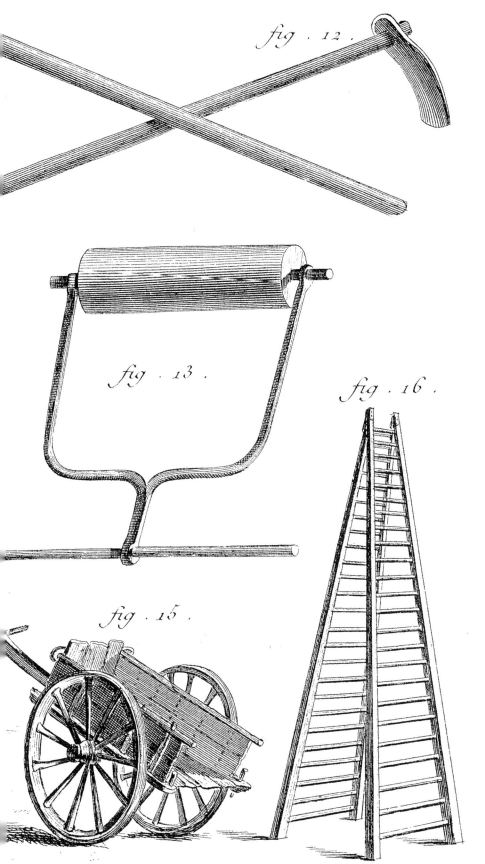

fig . 12 .

fig . 13 .

fig . 16 .

fig . 15 .

IX.
The Garden of Hateful Parents

Christina Stead
The Man Who Loved Children

[United States / Australia, 1940]

One of the most beautiful gardens ever written is located in the Washington, D.C. neighborhood of Georgetown—sort of. The two acres of Tohoga House—graced with the Native American name for Georgetown—at first seem to correspond more or less with those of a recognizable landmark, Century House, at 3406 R Street. Tohoga House is the home of Sam and Henny Pollit and their six, eventually seven children, the eldest of whom, Louie—Sam's child by his first marriage—will grow up to be, we assume, the author of this novel. In the course of the action we "see" little of the garden in descriptive terms. Although Sam is very proud of the house (and has pretentious plans to change its name to Tohoga Place), only a few of its features are actually of his philoprogenitive making: "the little Colorado blue spruce which he had planted for the children's 'Wishing Tree'" (running around it a designated number of times grants the wish) (p. 19)[18] and various children's gardens, including a rock garden, "wind-picked and weed-covered"; a cement fishpond; and cages for animals, including lots of snakes (pp. 260–70). Most of the garden's charm is simply due to nature: the "immense trees, full of birds and birds' nests" and the passing clouds, "swiftly staining the garden, the stains soaking in and leaving only bright light again" (p. 58). We also see the efforts of previous

owners: the "man-high hedges" (p. 47) and an orchard, of what it is not absolutely clear, although apples would seem logical.

For the Pollit children the garden of Tohoga House could well be a childhood paradise, but after we read a few pages it occurs to us that, paradise or not, this is the Garden of Eden after we humans have fucked it up. I use this puerile obscenity on purpose, for the distinguishing feature of Tohoga House is that it serves as the battlefield where the horrible sound of the war between the sexes reverberates across the landscape, poisoning the lives of the beloved children. Both Henny and Sam are bullies, she endlessly ranting about the ills that have been done her and why she'd be better off dead, he endlessly indulging in a self-serving and self-pitying plaint composed of invented words voiced in a dialect modeled on Mark Twain, Uncle Remus, and Artemus Ward (sort of Early Southern Hick). I do not quote on purpose. By the middle of the novel we are absolutely sick of hearing their voices, one of Stead's most brilliant narrative moves, for we feel how they must sound to the children, who hear them unceasingly every day, especially Louie—mercilessly bullied for her attempts at independence and her unattractive appearance. ("Shut

At Boongarre in Watson's Bay, Australia—where Stead spent her late childhood—a fence and a basketball hoop provide an appropriate symbolic entrance to a nightmare Eden.

83

up, shut up, shut up," she scrawls when her father thinks she is noting down his current words of wisdom.)

Interestingly enough, these voices are neither Washingtonian, nor more generally American, but Australian, a disjunction that serves a most important artistic purpose. The novel is based on Stead's childhood in Sydney, Australia, Tohoga House most clearly corresponding to Lydham Hill, the home of her early childhood (circa 1907 to 1917) in the Bexley-Arncliffe district of Rockdale, while Spa House in Annapolis, where the Pollits move mid-novel, is comparable to Boongarre in Watson's Bay, the home of Stead's later childhood and young adulthood (1917–1928). Both houses were located in poor districts. Lydham Hill had a garden of three and a half acres, Boongarre a large backyard that sloped down to the harbor. The land at both locations has now been developed beyond recognition. The novel takes place at the end of the 1930s, ten years later than the autobiographical model, because by the time she wrote it Stead realized she had lost touch with Australia. The time shift is, however, far less disconcerting—and artistically effective—than the geographic move. In the early twenty-first century we are not so sensitive to the difference between 1925 and 1935, but we "hear" almost immediately that the Pollits are not Americans and we realize that Stead's knowledge of Washington is slight to nonexistent. It is, really, a little hard for the reader to tell what the Pollits are or where they actually belong. Stead may have performed this crucial relocation, as she claimed, because she wanted to spare her family, but biographer Hazel Rowley writes that Simon & Schuster must have "insisted on it, persuading her that it would make the book more marketable for an American readership.[19] For whatever reason, this relocation makes the tale universal and transforms the specific Australian voices of Sam and Henny into the never-ending Freudian howl that echoes through everyone's childhood, wherever it took place and no matter how beautiful the surrounding plant life.

After Sam returns from a long trip to Singapore, the garden—largely, but not totally, appropriate to the District's climate—is distinguished by "lots of weeds" (p. 253): "The neglected garden thronged upwards with all its plants into the new sun, with its guava trees, peach trees, magnolia trees, apple trees, seedling pines and forsythia, and the wild double narcissus that grew so rank and green on the possums' graves" (p. 286). Soon we understand that the family itself is the principal weed. One of the chief Pollit problems is their lack of money —whether through extravagance or lack of planning or both. They live in Tohoga House rent-free because it is owned by Henny's father. After his death they must move to the unkempt, mean little Spa House near Annapolis, where their lives move into hand-to-mouth mode and we see virtually nothing of their physical surroundings. One suspects Stead needed to find a location near the water in order to write about specific autobiographical horrors, for example, the marlin (carefully substituted for the Australian Blue Pointer shark) that Sam reduces into useful by-products, a terrifying and disgusting scene in which we see Leviathan boiled down to oil.[20]

And yet, once again, a place (Uji in *The Tale of Genji*, the forest in *Alice in Wonderland*) demonstrates its value by not being a garden, for it is in the "wilderness" of Spa House that Louie comes into her own nature as a writer. Blessed with a sympathetic teacher, Miss Aiden, she calls her new school "Arcadia" (p. 337), never a term applicable to any aspect of Tohoga House. After the terrible denouement Louie finds herself "on the other side of a fence; there was a garden through the chinks that she had once been in, but could never be in again" (p. 517). Accepting the loss of Eden, she sets off "'for a walk round the world'" (p. 527). The Ugly Duckling has found her Pond.

X.
The Garden of Loving Literature

Vladimir Nabokov
Ada, or Ardor: A Family Chronicle

[United States, 1969]

To create one of the most beautifully maddening of
fictional gardens Nabokov jokingly substitutes culture
for nature. At Ardis Hall near Ladore in the northern
stretches of Anti-Terra brother and sister Van and Ada
Veen initiate a life-long love affair. The truly great love
affair that takes place at Ardis Hall is not, however,
theirs. Rather, *Ada* celebrates Nabokov's overwhelming
passion for literature as he transforms the estate from
a rather banal landscape into one heavily planted with
cleverly twisted allusions to French, Russian, English,
Italian, German, and American literature.

Perhaps the defining condition of Nabokov's garden is its
location in Anti-Terra, the world of fiction, which lags
behind the real world (Terra) by some fifty years. In
addition to literary allusions, the grounds of Ardis boast
many word games (at which Ada and Nabokov are particularly adept) and self-referential nods to *Ada* itself,
which is being written by Van and edited by Ada late in
their lives, shortly before they fade into the blurb on the
book jacket.

Throughout this guide I have used the device of the list
to shorten the text (as is the custom with guidebooks)
and to indicate a rhythm of significance that finds its basis

in the poetic line. The list is also a means of organiza-
tion, one that frequently serves to emphasize
an elemental absence of order. Such are the lists of
scattered garden elements and random literary jokes in
the garden of Ardis Hall. My own lists give but a taste of
Ada's elaborate literary game.

Nabokov amasses "actual" garden elements at Ardis
Hall. Some appear and reappear, while others seem
invented for a specific occasion. They include

a rose garden (p. 29)

a green bench under Persian lilacs (p. 36)

a paulownia tree (p. 43)

a line of larches (pp. 45, 129)

"a woman of marble bending over a . . . broken
jar" (pp. 50, 399)

a *rond-point* "encircled by flowerbeds and
jasmine bushes in heavy bloom" with a linden
stretching up to meet an oak (pp. 51, 398)

staked peonies (p. 51)

imperialis and liriodendron trees (p. 68), called
lidderons, "not exactly a *lit d'edredon* [eiderdown
bed] though worth an auroral pun" (p. 400)

the weeping cedar (pp. 72, 397), "whose aberrant limbs extended an oriental canopy (propped up here and there by crutches made of its own flesh like this book)" (p. 204)

"a picturesque glade in an old pinewood cut by ravishingly lovely ravines" (pp. 79, 266)

a rustic seat under an immense elm (p. 89)

a cascade within the larch grove (p. 140)

a forbidden garden pavilion used for lovemaking and reached via a grove and a grotto (pp. 148, 398)

laurels and lilies flanking the front porch (p. 189)

new kerosene-powered garden lamps with golden globes (p. 211)

a secret islet with "three Babylonian willows, a fringe of alder, many grasses, cattails, sweet-flags, and a few purple-lipped twayblades" (pp. 216-17)

a boxwood maze and bagatelle arches (p. 416).[21]

Does this scattering of features add up to a real garden? Or are they simply the conventional props for a literary

romance? Conceivably the only plant that makes a difference is the Shattal apple tree—on whose cool limb Ada "tried to assuage the rash in the soft arch" (p. 78). It is called the Tree of Knowledge and is rumored to have been "imported last summer . . . from the Eden National Park" in Iraq (p. 95).

The grounds of Ardis Hall inspire a few scattered references to painters— Toulouse-Lautrec and Caravaggio—but the most important graphic reference is an unreproduced collection of photographs taken by a blackmailer, an outrage that goads Van into writing *Ada* (p. 406). It is left to the reader to decipher a flood of puns, parodies, and off-beat literary references:

> Jane Austen's establishment-loving *Mansfield Park* (pp. 8, 231, 249, 405)

> *Eugene Onegin*, transmuted into a brainless musical comedy (pp. 11, 317, 481)

> Leo Tolstoy's *Anna Karenin* (p. 25, 26, 299, 323) —"When in early September Van Veen left Manhattan for Lute, he was pregnant" (p. 325); also *War and Peace* and *The Death of Ivan Ilyich* (p. 232)

> *Dr. Zhivago*, called "Les Amours du Docteur

Among the hundreds of plants mentioned in the text are: Liriodendron *(upper left)*; Weeping cedar *(lower left)*; Jacaranda *(upper right)*; and Imperialis *(lower right)*.

Mertvago," the root of "death" substituted for the root of "life" (p. 53)

Proust, "the Cattleya Hawkmoth" and "the Odettian Sphinx of the guermantoid type" (p. 57)

Chateaubriand's *Atala* (p. 89), *Ombres and coleurs* (p. 280), and the lines from *Romance à Helene* that provide a leit-motif in the novel: "*Oh! Qui me rendra mon Helene. Et ma montagne et le grand chêne*" (pp. 106, 133, 139, 596)

Turgenev's *Fathers and Children* (p. 105)

Chekhov's *The Cherry Orchard* (p. 115), *Uncle Vanya* (p. 193), *The Seagull* (p. 272), and *Four Sisters* (p. 427)

Moliére's *Tartuffe* (p. 117)

Floebert's *Ursula* (Flaubert's *Madame Bovary*) (p. 128)

Rabelais and Casanova (whom Van and Ada like), Sade, Masoch, and Heinrich Muller (whom they loathe) (p. 136)

Goethe, d'Annunzio (pp. 152–53)

Lermontov (pp. 171, 180)

Pushkin (p. 171)

H.G. Wells's *Invisible Man* (p. 203)

Walter Scott, Dickens, and Dostoevsky
(pp. 240, 360)

Jules Verne (p. 334)

Cyrano de Bergerac (p. 339)

Burton's translation of Nefzawi's
Perfumed Garden (p. 344)

La Condition Humaine, translated as
The Manly State (p. 377)

The Faerie Queene, (p. 418)

What Daisy Knew (p. 512)

Ogden Nash, "The Veens speak only to
Tobaks / But the Tobaks speak only to dogs
(p. 456).

There is also the governess, Mademoiselle Lariviere,
who writes all of Maupassant's work and wins the Lebon
Academy Prize "for her copious rubbish" (p. 456).

The novel includes many word games with garden
references:

Marvell's "The Garden" in French (p. 65)

Ada's take on Lear

    Ce beau jardin fleurit en mai,
    Mais en hiver
    Jamais, jamais, jamais, jamais, jamais
    N'est vert; n'est vert, n'est vert, n'est vert
    n'est vert (p. 92)

Ada's sexual exploration of Van: "'The cap of the Red Bolete is not half as plushy. In fact . . . I'm reminded of geranium or rather pelargonium bloom'" (p. 119); captured along with "another interesting plant, Marvell's Melon, imitating the backside of an occupied lad" (p. 405)

Fall—"the last resort of nature, felicitous alliterations (when flowers and flies mime one another)" (p. 139)

a code based on the seventy-two lines of Marvell's "The Garden" and the forty lines of Rimbaud's "Memoire" (p. 161)

the most beautiful of all anagrams: "Eros, the rose and the sore" (pp. 351, 367).

Ada also includes many self-references:

    Ada's poem to Van in Van's voice:

      In the old manor, I've parodied
      Every veranda and room,

And jacarandas at Arrowhead
In supernatural bloom (p. 324)

the birth of local legend—"Romantically inclined
handmaids . . . adored Van, adored Ada, adored
Ardis's ardors in arbors. Their swains, plucking
ballads on their seven-stringed Russian lyres
under the racemosa in bloom or in old rose
gardens . . . added freshly composed lines. . . .
Gardeners paraphrased iridescent Persian poems
about irrigation and the Four Arrows of Love.
Nightwatchmen fought insomnia and the fire
of the clap with the weapons of *Vaniada's
Adventures.*" (p. 409)

Van's "only contribution to Anglo-American
poetry"—one line of a poem, "Ada, our ardors
and arbors" (p. 74).

Need the beautiful gardens of Ardis be composed of
anything other than literary references?

Coda:
The Writer's Garden,
The Reader's Garden

Now, really, you may ask, are the gardens discussed in this guidebook beautiful or simply maddening? A fair question because in each novel what we are able to imagine—with some difficulty—as the physical beauty of the garden, a garden made and maintained by human will and activity, is undermined by the examples of human activity taking place in its confines. Indeed, the writer exaggerates this undermining behavior to create the very form of the fictional garden. Such is the craft of fiction, shamelessly using whatever comes to hand to advance its own effects. Consider:

Genji's mansion and grounds, which justify ceremonial religion and conventional social structures as well as institutional polygamy

the distant garden Isle of Cytherea, where Poliphilo is denied Polia's love

the very material location of Hsi-men Ch'ing's greed and physical indulgence

the Jias' prospectless garden that proclaims the curse of nature

Uncle Toby's fortifications against life and love

Eduard's estate, always being improved, never improving

Alice's garden of nasty humanlike flowers

poor Bouvard and Pécuchet's stylish garden of popular middle-class stupidities

the Pollits' battleground

the Veens' estate, which presumably celebrates love, but really celebrates a love of literature as expressed by incessant jokes.

In every case we must remind ourselves that the Garden of Eden was not just the physically beautiful site of Paradise, skillfully maintained by Adam and Eve. It was also the place where Paradise was lost, its every twig and leaf configured by an innocence that had to be sacrificed so that mankind could achieve consciousness . . . so that mankind could become unpleasantly human.

As the reader of this guidebook you may legitimately ask: What, after all, am I being guided to see? What do these gardens actually look like? Where do these gardens really come from? What do they have to do with real gardens? First, a partial answer: It seems safe to say that the gardens as they were originally imagined by the writers probably resembled the gardens they saw around them every day. These would also have been familiar to their initial readers, those Heian court ladies and Ming intellectuals, those eighteenth-, nineteenth-, and twentieth-century Chinese, English, French, German, Australian, and American devourers of prose fiction. When a writer mentioned a garden, the initial readers could look around them and see what a garden looked like. As for us later readers, flipping through the books listed in the Garden Bibliography can give some idea of the relevant historical gardens—at least as imagined and recorded by artists and photographers. And reading the text of these histories will give a more detailed guide to the achievements of real-world garden designers and the desires of their clients, a relationship that garners a harsh assessment in these novels. Consider:

> Genji designs his gardens but delegates the work
>
> Hsi-men pays but does nothing else
>
> the Jias delegate design, maintenance, and interpretation
>
> Uncle Toby has Trim do the work
>
> aside from Eduard's failed grafts, the fabulous four delegate all work other than design
>
> Bouvard and Pécuchet imagine hired help and fail on their own
>
> Sam Pollit puts his kids to work
>
> the other gardens simply appear in an inexplicably finished state.

Well, so much for historical reality. What do the gardens of these novels mean to us, right now? Where do the sensations that are the soul of the real garden come from when we encounter a garden on the page? Happily, whatever text we are handed, we readers bring our own memories to the party. For example, whenever I read about a cherry tree—in Genji's garden, for example, in Murasaki's southeast quarter, which celebrates spring and love—my reading of the words on the page mingles with the memory of the cherry tree in the backyard of the house my parents rented on South Dicks Street in Muncie, Indiana, from the time I was ten until I was thirteen. Genji's cherry tree merges with the scent and the sight of that tree, because that was the cherry tree I could smell, that was the cherry tree I could see. And as I read of its existence, Murasaki's cherry tree is infused with the taste of the cherry preserves my grandmother made every year from the fruit of that tree, infused as well with the vision of Lee Cooper, a boy my own age, who lived next door and mowed the lawn and picked the real cherries and was the most handsome man I have ever known, a Genji of sorts, you might say.

In the end the fictional garden may be so beautiful because whatever the writer's intentions, it revives and amplifies and puts into a broader context our very own memories of our very own garden.

1   Court lady and novelist Murasaki Shikibu, whose real name we do not know, is designated by the name of her most popular female character. Modern texts of *The Tale of Genji* are taken from a 1225 redaction by Fujiwara no Teika. In his footnotes, translator Royall Tyler brilliantly explains the poetic allusions that govern plants, plant products, landscape forms, garden-based ceremonies, and weather (New York: Viking, 2001).

2   A good source of information about the historical Heian mansion is Ivan Morris, *The World of the Shining Prince: Court Life in Ancient Japan* (New York: A. A. Knopf, 1964). A particularly important document for understanding Murasaki Shikibu's fictional exploitation of the garden is the eleventh-century treatise written by Heian aristocrat Tachibana no Toshitsuna (1028–1094) to accompany the oral instruction given to aristocrats and priests who wanted to design gardens, *Sakuteiki: Visions of the Japanese Garden: A Modern Translation of Japan's Gardening Classic*, trans. Jiro Takai and Marc P. Keane (Boston: Tuttle Publishing, 2001).

3   Noting that the role of these festivals in the lives of Heian aristocrats "can hardly be exaggerated,"

Morris lists thirty-three quasi-religious ceremonies and festivals in the court calendar. Many are linked to plants and in the case of Shinto rituals have an origin in the agricultural cycle.

4   Translated by Joscelyn Godwin (London: Thames & Hudson, 1999), p. xvi. John Dixon Hunt, *The Afterlife of Gardens* (Philadelphia: University of Pennsylvania Press, 2004), p. 61.

5   Godwin, p. ix.

6   Background information comes from David Tod Roy's introduction to *Volume One: The Gathering*, xxxix. The other volumes include *Volume Two: The Rivals, Volume Three: The Aphrodisiac, Volume Four: The Climax,* and *Volume Five: The Dissolution* (Princeton: Princeton University Press, 1993–2013). For *Chin P'ing Mei* and *The Story of the Stone* spelling follows the translators' versions.

7   The imperial garden was filled with rocks collected from all over China by the "Patterned Rock Convoy," whose methods of extortion —along with the expense of the garden—led to the fall of the Northern Sung, Andrew Plaks, *The Four Masterworks of the Ming Novel* (Princeton: Princeton University Press,

1987), pp. 162-63, and Ji Cheng. *The Craft of Gardens*, trans. Alison Hardie (New Haven: Yale University Press, 1988), p. 134, note 162.

8   Translated by David Hawkes, *Volume One: The Golden Days*, *Volume Two: The Crab-Flower Club*, and *Volume Three: The Warning Voice*; translated by John Minford, *Volume Four: The Debt of Tears* and *Volume Five: The Dreamer Wakes*. (London: Penguin, 1973–1986).

9   Hawkes, Introduction, I, 23–32.

10   *Archetype and Allegory in The Dream of the Red Chamber* (Princeton: Princeton University Press, 1976), pp. 153-54.

11   Cao disguises the fact that the women in *The Story of the Stone* are Manchu women, whose feet were not bound—unlike those of the aristocratic Han, Hawkes, Introduction, I, 24, note 4. The distances in the novel register the perception of women with bound feet and thus perpetuate Cao's imaginative social climbing.

12   (New York: Penguin, 1978).

13   Translated by David Constantine (Oxford: Oxford University Press, 1994).

14   (New York: Penguin, 1998).

15   Carroll loves to make fun of serious poems. The flowers are descended from those in Tennyson's *Maud* (1855).

16   Hugh Haughton, Introduction (London: Penguin, 1998), pp. lxxviff.

17   Translated by A.J. Krailsheimer (London: Penguin, 1976).

18   (New York: Henry Holt, 1968).

19   Hazel Rowley reports that Stead and her husband William Blech (pseudonym, William Blake) spent lots of time searching for locations in Washington and Baltimore, *Christina Stead: A Biography* (New York: Henry Holt, 1993), pp. 260-61ff. Rowley gives no evidence for her speculation that the change of location was at the request of the publisher.

20   Rowley, p. 36.

21   (New York: Vintage, 1990).

Illustrations

Of the ten novels, *Hypnerotomachia Poliphili*, a seventeenth-century edition of *Chin P'ing Mei*, and Carroll's Alice novels include graphic depictions. For the most part the beauty of the gardens in all ten novels is primarily conveyed to the reader by the devices of fiction. Illustrations have been chosen to reflect this fact.

I. Murasaki Shikibu,
The Tale of Genji

Kagero (The Drake Fly)
attributed to Tosa Mitsuoki
(1617-1691)
[Mary and Jackson Burke Collection,
Metropolitan Museum,
of Art, New York]

II: Francesco Colonna,
Hypnerotomachia Poliphili,
p. 195

III: [T'ang Hsien-tsu].
Chin P'ing Mei, II, 147

IV. Cao Xueqin,
The Story of the Stone

[Photograph by Peter Walker]

V: Laurence Sterne,
The Life and Opinions of Tristram Shandy, Gentleman

[Photograph by Jacques Verroust, in Ian Hogg,
The History of Fortification
(New York: St. Martin's Press, 1981), p. 124]

VI: Johann Wolfgang von Goethe,
Elective Affinities

Humphry Repton's business card.
[courtesy Stephen Daniels]

VII: Lewis Carroll,
Alice's Adventures in Wonderland
and *Through the Looking-Glass
and What Alice Found There*

Drawings by John Tenniel from the
Illustrated Junior Library edition
(New York: Grosset and Dunlap,
1946), pp. 168, 188]

'Oh, Tiger-Lily,' said Alice, 'I wish you could talk!'

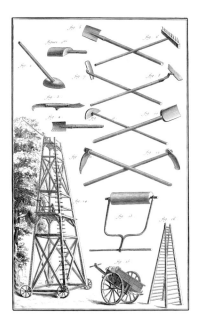

VIII.   Gustave Flaubert,
Bouvard and Pécuchet

[Plate 5, Gardening I,
from Denis Diderot,
*L'Encyclopédie, ou Dictionnaire
Raisonné des Sciences, des Arts
et des Métiers* [1763],
Charles C. Gillispie, ed.
(New York: Dover Publications,
Inc., 1959)]

IX.   Christina Stead,
The Man Who Loved Children
[Photograph by Peter Walker]

X. Vladimir Nabokov,
Ada, or Ardor: A Family Chronicle

Internet portraits of:
a. Liriodenron (*Ada*, p. 400)
b. Weeping cedar (*Ada*, p. 204)
c. Jacaranda (*Ada*, p. 524)
d. Imperialis (*Ada*, p. 400)

Garden Bibliography

I. Murasaki Shikibu, *The Tale of Genji*

Sakuteiki: Visions of the Japanese Garden: A Modern Translation of Japan's Gardening Classic, trans. Jiro Takai and Marc P. Keane. Boston: Tuttle Publishing, 2001. Eleventh-century text with a variety of graphics

The Tale of Genji: Legends and Paintings. New York: George Braziller, 2001. Fifty-four paintings from the Burke albums "attributed to Tosa Mitsuoki (1617-1691) but probably by an anonymous artist of the Tosa school"

The Tale of Genji Scroll. Tokyo: Kodansha International, 1971. Twenty sections of a twelfth-century scroll

II. Francesco Colonna, *Hypnerotomachia Poliphili*

Michel Cambornac. *Plantes et jardins du moyen age.* Paris: Hartmann Edition, 2003.

Sylvia Landsberg. *The Medieval Garden.* London: British Museum, 1995.

Marilyn Stokstad and Jerry Stannard. *Gardens of the Middle Ages.* Lawrence: University of Kansas, 1983.

III. [T'ang Hsien-tsu], *Chin P'ing Mei*
IV. Cao Xueqin, *The Story of the Stone*

Cheng Liyao. *Ancient Chinese Architecture: Imperial Gardens*, trans. Zhang Long. New York: Springer-Verlag Wien, 1998.

_____. *Ancient Chinese Architecture: Private Gardens*, trans. Zhang Long. New York: Springer-Verlag Wien, 1999.

Hu Jie. *The Splendid Chinese Garden: Origins, Aesthetics and Architecture*, trans. Li Yan. New York: Better Link Press, 2013.

Ji Cheng. *The Craft of Gardens*, trans. Alison Hardie. New Haven: Yale University Press, 1988. Originally published, 1631

V. Laurence Stern, *The Life and Times of Tristram Shandy, Gentleman*
VII. Lewis Carroll, *Alice's Adventures in Wonderland* and *Through the Looking-Glass*

Edward Hyams. *The English Garden*. New York: Harry N. Abrams, 1968.

Charles Quest-Ritson. *The English Garden: A Social History*. Boston: David R. Godine, 2003.

Tom Turner. *English Garden Design: History and styles since 1650*. Woodbridge, England: Antique Collectors' Club, 1986.

VI. Johann Wolfgang von Goethe, *Elective Affinities*

C.C.L. Hirschfeld. *Theory of Garden Art*, trans. Linda B.
Parshall. Philadelphia: University of Pennsylvania, 2001.
Originally published in five volumes, 1779-1785

Hermann Puckler-Muskau. *Hints on Landscape Gardening*,
trans. Bernhard Sickert. Boston: Houghton Mifflin, 1917.
Written mid-nineteenth-century

VIII. Gustave Flaubert, *Bouvard and Pécuchet*

L. E. Audot. *Traite de la composition et de l'ornement des
Jardins*. Paris: L.V.D.V. Inter-livres, 1859.

Pierre Boitard. *L'Art de Composer et Decorer les Jardins*.
New York: Hachette, 2013.
Originally published, 1834

Jean de Cayeux. *Hubert Robert et les Jardins*. Paris:
Editions Herscher, 1987.

IX. Christina Stead, *The Man Who Loved Children*

Richard Aitken. *Gardenesque: A Celebration of Australian
Gardens*. Melbourne: The Miegunyah Press, 2004.

Georgina Whitehead, ed. *Planting the Nation*.
Melbourne: Australian Garden History Society, 2001.

X. Vladimir Nabokov, *Ada, or Ardor: A Family Chronicle*

Mac Griswold and Eleanor Weller. *The Golden Age of American Gardens: Proud Owners, Private Estates, 1890-1940*. New York: Harry N. Abrams, 2000.

Robin Karson. *A Genius for Place: American Landscapes of the Country Place Era*. Amherst: University of Massachusetts Press, 2007.

R. Terry Schnadelbach. *Ferruccio Vitale: Landscape Architect of the Country Place Era*. New York: Princeton Architectural Press, 2001.

Literary Bibliography

Cao Xueqin. *The Story of the Stone, or The Dream of the Red Chamber*, trans. David Hawkes and John Minford. London: Penguin, 1973-1986.

Lewis Carroll. *Alice's Adventures in Wonderland* and *Through the Looking-Glass and What Alice Found There*. London: Penguin, 1998.

Francesco Colonna. *Hypnerotomachia Poliphili*, trans. Joscelyn Godwin. London: Thames & Hudson, 1999.

Gustave Flaubert. *Bouvard and Pécuchet*, trans. A.J. Krailsheimer. London: Penguin, 1976.

Johann Wolfgang von Goethe. *Elective Affinities*, trans. David Constantine. Oxford: Oxford University Press, 1994.

John Dixon Hunt. *The Afterlife of Gardens*. Philadelphia: University of Pennsylvania Press, 2004.

Ivan Morris. *The World of the Shining Prince: Court Life in Ancient Japan*. New York: A. A. Knopf, 1964.

Murasaki Shikibu. *The Tale of Genji*, trans. Royall Tyler. New York: Viking, 2001.

Vladimir Nabokov. *Ada, or Ardor: A Family Chronicle.*
New York: Vintage, 1990.

Andrew Plaks. *Archetype and Allegory in The Dream of the Red Chamber.* Princeton: Princeton University Press, 1976.

_____. *The Four Masterworks of the Ming Novel: Ssu ta ch'i-shu.* Princeton: Princeton University Press, 1988.

Hazel Rowley. *Christina Stead: A Biography.* New York: Henry Holt, 1993.

Christina Stead. *The Man Who Loved Children.*
New York: Henry Holt, 1968.

Laurence Stern. *The Life and Opinions of Tristram Shandy, Gentleman.* New York: Penguin, 1978.

[T'ang Hsien-tsu]. *Chin P'ing Mei, or The Plum in the Golden Vase,* trans. David Tod Roy. Princeton: Princeton Library of Asian Translations, 1993-2013.